The Cookbook of Everything C

Flavorful Recipes to Recreate a Restaurant Favorite at Home

BY: SOPHIA FREEMAN

© 2021 Sophia Freeman All Rights Reserved

COPYRIGHTED

Liability

This publication is meant as an informational tool. The individual purchaser accepts all liability if damages occur because of following the directions or guidelines set out in this publication. The Author bears no responsibility for reparations caused by the misuse or misinterpretation of the content.

Copyright

The content of this publication is solely for entertainment purposes and is meant to be purchased by one individual. Permission is not given to any individual who copies, sells or distributes parts or the whole of this publication unless it is explicitly given by the Author in writing.

Table of Contents

Introduction 6

Additional Useful & Interesting Information 8

    Chicken Curry 9

    Chickpea & Quinoa Curry 13

    Thai Chicken Curry 16

    Coconut Chicken Curry Noodle Soup 19

    Chicken Curry Salad Sandwich 23

    Lentil Curry 26

    Peanut Pork Curry 29

    Roasted Curried Cauliflower & Chickpeas 32

    Turkey Curry 35

    Sweet & Sour Chicken Curry 38

    Chicken Curry with Pineapple 41

    Coconut Curry Shrimp 45

    Pork & Apple Curry 48

    Lamb & Potato Curry 51

    Chicken & Corn Chowder Curry 55

    Vegetable Thai Curry Soup 58

    Tofu & Cauliflower Curry 61

    Caribbean Chicken Curry 64

Red Chicken Curry	68
Filipino-Style Chicken Curry	71
Turkey & Cauliflower Curry	75
Spicy Chicken Curry	78
Chicken & Veggie Curry	82
Curry Pork Chops with Tomato	85
Cauliflower Curry with Chickpeas & Green Peas	88
Curried Chicken Meatballs in Lettuce Wraps	91
Curried Quinoa Salad	94
Chicken Curry Turnovers	97
Rice & Noodle Curry	100
Peach & Curried Chicken Salad	103
Potato & Chickpea Curry	106
Coconut Red Curry Stew	110
Curry Chicken & Rice	114
Slow Cooked Pork Curry	117
Egg Curry Salad Sandwich	120
Sausage & Squash Curry	123
Shrimp & Pineapple Curried Fried Rice	126
Curried Beef Stew	129
Chicken Curry Lasagna	133
Curried Eggs & Rice	137

Chicken Tikka Masala 140

Crispy Curry Chicken 144

Chicken Curry Zucchini Noodle Soup 147

Eggplant Curry 151

Curry Roast Chicken 154

Creamy Vegetable Curry 158

Chicken & Sweet Potato Curry 161

Butter Chicken 164

Curry Sausages 168

Turkey & Sweet Potato Curry 171

Conclusion 174

About the Author 175

Author's Afterthoughts 176

Introduction

Curry is a food that is highly popular yet also largely misunderstood. The most common misconceptions being that curry is too spicy, oily, complicated to prepare and time-consuming to cook.

The truth is, cooking curry dishes is so much more than just sprinkling a generous amount of curry powder into a pot of ingredients and then calling it a day. In fact, the term "curry" actually refers to any dish that has meat, poultry, fish, or vegetables that are cooked in a gravy flavored with aromatic spices and herbs.

Traditional curry is characterized by making things from scratch and involves fresh ingredients, which translates to healthy food devoid of any preservatives. Another plus factor is that the herbs and spices required to create the gravy for curry are packed with healing and medicinal properties.

There are many surprising combinations for ingredients that may go into a curry dish, and this ultimately results in a very pleasant interplay of spicy, salty, sour, bitter, sweet and tangy flavors that appeal to any discerning palate.

Additional Useful & Interesting Information

It's not necessarily true that curry dishes are always too hot and spicy. The great thing about cooking your own curry dishes is that you can adjust according to your preference and omit ingredients like chili that actually bring out heat in a dish without sacrificing the flavors of other spices.

Health-conscious individuals will be pleasantly surprised to find that there are many curry recipes that call for very little or no oil at all. By boiling, steaming, roasting or grilling the ingredients, you can achieve genuine curry flavors minus the added fat.

Chicken Curry

Slow cooking your chicken curry results in chicken that's not only fall-off-the-bone tender but also infused with incredible flavors, giving your taste buds an unforgettable treat.

Serving Size: 6

Preparation & Cooking Time: 5 hours

Ingredients:

- 6 chicken breast fillets
- 1 ¼ teaspoons salt
- Cooking spray
- 14 oz. coconut milk
- ½ teaspoon ground turmeric
- ½ teaspoon cayenne pepper
- 1 teaspoon curry powder
- 2 green onions, chopped
- 2 tablespoons cornstarch
- 2 tablespoons cold water
- 2 tablespoons lime juice

For serving

- Chopped green onions
- 3 cups hot cooked rice

Instructions:

Season the chicken with the salt.

Spray your pan with oil.

Place it over medium heat.

Cook the chicken until browned on both sides.

Transfer to your slow cooker.

In a bowl, mix the coconut milk, ground turmeric, cayenne pepper and curry powder.

Pour the mixture over the chicken.

Top with the green onions.

Cover the pot.

Cook on low for 4 hours.

Mix water and cornstarch in a bowl.

Add the mixture to the slow cooker.

Cover and cook on high for 30 minutes

Stir in the lime juice.

Sprinkle the green onions on top of the chicken.

Serve the chicken curry with the hot cooked rice.

Nutrients per Serving:

- Calories 353
- Fat 9 g
- Saturated fat 5 g
- Carbohydrates 27 g
- Fiber 1 g
- Protein 37 g
- Cholesterol 94 mg
- Sugars 2 g
- Sodium 576 mg
- Potassium 402 mg

Chickpea & Quinoa Curry

Enjoy a bowl of flavorful curry made with quinoa and chickpeas. This is a protein-packed meal that also gives you luscious flavors and cheerful colors that certainly brighten up the dinner table.

Serving Size: 4

Preparation & Cooking Time: 45 minutes

Ingredients:

- ½ cup orange juice
- 1 ½ cups water
- 1 red onion, minced
- 2 tomatoes, chopped
- 1 sweet red pepper, sliced into strips
- 1 cup quinoa, rinsed and drained
- 15 oz. chickpeas, rinsed and drained
- 1 teaspoon curry powder
- ½ cup raisins
- ½ cup fresh cilantro, minced

Instructions:

Pour the orange juice and water into a pan over medium heat.

Bring to a boil.

Stir in the rest of the ingredients except the cilantro.

Reduce heat.

Cover and simmer for 20 minutes.

Turn off heat.

Fluff using a fork.

Top with the cilantro and serve.

Nutrients per Serving:

- Calories 355
- Fat 5 g
- Saturated fat 0 g
- Carbohydrates 70 g
- Fiber 9 g
- Protein 12 g
- Cholesterol 0 mg
- Sugars 20 g
- Sodium 155 mg
- Potassium 803 mg

Thai Chicken Curry

If you love Thai food, you're in for a treat. This Thai chicken curry dish is flavorful, creamy, and spicy—it's everything you love in a curry dish. Amp up the heat with chili powder if you like.

Serving Size: 4

Preparation & Cooking Time: 30 minutes

Ingredients:

- 1 lb. chicken breast fillet, sliced into cubes
- Salt and pepper to taste
- 1 tablespoon olive oil
- 1 clove garlic, minced
- 6 green onions, chopped
- 1 ½ cups chicken stock
- 2 tablespoons cornstarch
- ¾ cup coconut milk
- 1 teaspoon low sodium soy sauce
- 1 tablespoon lime juice
- 1 teaspoon red curry paste

For serving

- ¼ cup coconut flakes (unsweetened)
- 2 cups cooked rice

Instructions:

Season the chicken cubes with the salt and pepper.

Pour the oil into a pan over medium high heat.

Cook the chicken for 3 minutes or until browned.

Stir in the garlic and onion.

Cook for 1 minute, stirring often.

In a bowl, mix the chicken stock and cornstarch.

Add this mixture to the pan.

Pour in the coconut milk, soy sauce and lime juice.

Stir in the red curry paste.

Bring to a boil.

Reduce heat and simmer for 5 minutes.

Top the curry with the coconut flakes and serve with the rice.

Nutrients per Serving:

- Calories 358
- Fat 13 g
- Saturated fat 6 g
- Carbohydrates 31 g
- Fiber 3 g
- Protein 28 g
- Cholesterol 63 mg
- Sugars 3 g
- Sodium 635 mg
- Potassium 467 mg

Coconut Chicken Curry Noodle Soup

This is a curry dish, a Thai dish, and chicken noodle soup in one bowl! Expect a beautiful blend of flavors and colors. You and your family will surely be enticed.

Serving Size: 6

Preparation & Cooking Time: 1 hour

Ingredients:

- 28 oz. coconut milk
- ½ cup red curry paste
- 8 oz. rice noodles
- 28 oz. chicken broth
- 2 tablespoons fish sauce
- ¾ teaspoon garlic salt
- ¼ cup brown sugar
- 3 cups rotisserie chicken, shredded
- ¾ cup bean sprouts
- 1 ½ cups carrot, shredded
- 1 ½ cups cabbage, shredded

Garnish

- Fresh cilantro
- Fresh basil

Instructions:

Pour the coconut milk into a pan over medium heat.

Bring to a boil.

Reduce heat.

Cover and cook for 10 minutes or until reduced.

Stir in the curry paste.

Cook while stirring to dissolve the curry paste.

Prepare the rice noodles according to the directions in the package.

Drain the noodles and set aside.

Pour in the broth and fish sauce.

Add the garlic salt and brown sugar.

Return to a boil.

Reduce heat and simmer for 10 minutes.

Stir in the chicken.

Cook for 3 minutes.

Add the noodles to serving bowls.

Pour the soup into the noodles.

Add the vegetables on top.

Garnish with the cilantro and basil.

Nutrients per Serving:

- Calories 601
- Fat 34 g
- Saturated fat 26 g
- Carbohydrates 50 g
- Fiber 4 g
- Protein 27 g
- Cholesterol 65 mg
- Sugars 12 g
- Sodium 1722 mg
- Potassium 653 mg

Chicken Curry Salad Sandwich

The secret to this sandwich recipe is mixing the salad the night before. This gives the mixture enough time for the flavors to wonderfully meld. The result: a hearty and filling sandwich loaded with flavors you can't get enough of.

Serving Size: 6

Preparation & Cooking Time: 20 minutes

Ingredients:

- 2 cups chicken breast, cooked and sliced into cubes
- ½ cup celery, chopped
- ¾ cup dried cranberries, sliced
- ¾ cup apple, diced
- ½ cup walnuts, chopped
- ¾ cup mayonnaise
- 2 teaspoons lemon juice
- 1 teaspoon curry powder
- 1 tablespoon green onion, chopped
- 6 lettuce leaves
- 6 croissants, sliced in half

Instructions:

Combine the chicken, celery, dried cranberries, apple, walnuts, mayo, lemon juice, curry powder and green onion in a bowl.

Add the lettuce on top of the croissant bottoms.

Scoop the chicken salad on top of the lettuce.

Replace with croissant tops.

Nutrients per Serving:

- Calories 625
- Fat 41 g
- Saturated fat 10 g
- Carbohydrates 43 g
- Fiber 4 g
- Protein 21 g
- Cholesterol 84 mg
- Sugars 14 g
- Sodium 614 mg
- Potassium 228 mg

Lentil Curry

This soup is a cross between chili and curry. You'll love the flavors and texture of this dish, and the comfort it brings you on a cold night.

Serving Size: 10

Preparation & Cooking Time: 8 hours and 15 minutes

Ingredients:

- 4 cups water
- 1 onion, chopped
- 2 cloves garlic, minced
- 1 celery rib, chopped
- 3 potatoes, diced
- 3 carrots, diced
- 28 oz. canned crushed tomatoes
- 1 cup dried lentils, rinsed
- 4 teaspoons curry powder
- 2 bay leaves
- 1 ¼ teaspoons salt

Instructions:

Add all the ingredients to your slow cooker.

Mix well.

Cover the pot.

Cook on low for 8 hours.

Discard the bay leaves before serving.

Nutrients per Serving:

- Calories 148
- Fat 1 g
- Saturated fat 0 g
- Carbohydrates 31 g
- Fiber 5 g
- Protein 7 g
- Cholesterol 0 mg
- Sugars 6 g
- Sodium 462 mg
- Potassium 534 mg

Peanut Pork Curry

Curry dishes are so versatile you can enhance them even more by adding other ingredients not typically used in curries like peanut butter, for example. Enjoy this peanut pork curry that tastes great.

Serving Size: 4

Preparation & Cooking Time: 35 minutes

Ingredients:

- 2 pork tenderloin, sliced into cubes
- Salt and pepper to taste
- 1 tablespoon olive oil
- 1 onion, chopped
- 2 cloves garlic, minced
- 1 cup carrots, sliced
- 1 cup chicken broth
- 14 ½ oz. canned diced tomatoes
- ½ cup peanut butter
- 1 cup coconut milk
- ¼ teaspoon cayenne pepper
- 3 teaspoons curry powder

Instructions:

Season the pork with the salt and pepper.

Add the oil to a pan over medium high heat.

Cook the pork for 5 minutes, stirring often.

Transfer to a plate.

In the same pan, cook the onion, garlic and carrot for 5 minutes, stirring.

Add the pork back to the pan.

Pour in the chicken broth and tomatoes.

Reduce heat and simmer for 5 minutes.

Add the peanut butter and coconut milk.

Season with the cayenne pepper and curry powder.

Simmer for 2 minutes.

Nutrients per Serving:

- Calories 463
- Fat 24 g
- Saturated fat 9 g
- Carbohydrates 36 g
- Fiber 4 g
- Protein 29 g
- Cholesterol 64 mg
- Sugars 29 g
- Sodium 837 mg
- Potassium 822 mg

Roasted Curried Cauliflower & Chickpeas

You don't have to be a vegetarian to enjoy this simple but appetizing dish made with cauliflower and chickpeas flavored with curry and roasted in the oven.

Serving Size: 4

Preparation & Cooking Time: 45 minutes

Ingredients:

- 15 oz. chickpeas, rinsed and drained
- 3 cups cauliflower florets
- 4 potatoes, sliced into cubes
- 3 tablespoons olive oil
- 2 teaspoons curry powder
- 3 tablespoons parsley, minced
- Salt and pepper to taste

Instructions:

Preheat your oven to 400 degrees F.

Toss chickpeas, cauliflower florets and potatoes in olive oil.

Sprinkle with curry power, parsley, salt and pepper.

Roast the vegetables inside the oven for 30 minutes, stirring once or twice.

Nutrients per Serving:

- Calories 339
- Fat 13 g
- Saturated fat 2 g
- Carbohydrates 51 g
- Fiber 8 g
- Protein 8 g
- Cholesterol 0 mg
- Sugars 6 g
- Sodium 605 mg
- Potassium 995 mg

Turkey Curry

If you have leftover turkey from last night's dinner, here's a delicious idea that you'd definitely want to try—savory turkey curry with carrots, dried onion, and celery.

Serving Size: 4

Preparation & Cooking Time: 20 minutes

Ingredients:

- Cooking spray
- ½ cup carrots, sliced
- 1 cup celery, sliced
- 2 tablespoons cornstarch
- 1 cup nonfat milk, divided
- ¾ cup low sodium chicken broth
- 2 cups turkey, cooked and sliced into cubes
- 2 tablespoons dried onion, minced
- ½ teaspoon garlic powder
- 4 teaspoons curry powder

For serving

- Hot cooked rice

Instructions:

Spray your pan with oil.

Add the carrots and celery to the pan.

Place it over medium heat.

Cook the vegetables for 3 minutes, stirring often.

In a bowl, mix the cornstarch and ¼ cup milk. Set aside.

Mix the remaining milk and broth.

Pour the broth mixture into the pan.

Bring to a boil.

Reduce heat and simmer for 2 minutes.

Stir in the cooked turkey.

Add the onion, curry powder and garlic powder.

Cook while stirring for 3 minutes.

Serve with the cooked rice.

Nutrients per Serving:

- Calories 172
- Fat 3 g
- Saturated fat 1 g
- Carbohydrates 12 g
- Fiber 1 g
- Protein 24 g
- Cholesterol 72 mg
- Sugars 5 g
- Sodium 235 mg
- Potassium 455 mg

Sweet & Sour Chicken Curry

This is not your typical curry dish that's dominant on the spice flavor, this one is a perfect balance of sweet, sour and spicy! For sure, you'll enjoy it.

Serving Size: 4

Preparation & Cooking Time: 4 hours and 45 minutes

Ingredients:

- 1 lb. chicken breast, sliced into cubes
- 1 onion, sliced
- 1 green pepper, sliced
- 14 ½ oz. canned stewed tomatoes
- 1 ½ teaspoons curry powder
- ½ cup mango chutney
- 2 tablespoons cornstarch
- ¼ cup cold water

Instructions:

Combine the chicken breast cubes, onion, green pepper, tomatoes, curry powder and mango chutney in your slow cooker.

Cover the pot.

Cook on low for 4 hours.

Mix the cornstarch and water in a bowl.

Add the mixture into the pot.

Cover the pot.

Cook on high for 30 minutes.

Nutrients per Serving:

- Calories 314
- Fat 3 g
- Saturated fat 1 g
- Carbohydrates 46 g
- Fiber 3 g
- Protein 25 g
- Cholesterol 63 mg
- Sugars 26 g
- Sodium 583 mg
- Potassium 767 mg

Chicken Curry with Pineapple

Pineapple adds interesting flavor to this chicken curry dish that's not only creamy and delicious but also bright and colorful!

Serving Size: 6

Preparation & Cooking Time: 6 hours and 30 minutes

Ingredients:

- 16 oz. canned pineapple chunks, undrained
- 6 chicken breast fillets, sliced into cubes
- 1 onion, sliced
- 1 sweet red pepper, sliced into strips
- 1 cup carrots, sliced into strips
- 15 oz. chickpeas, rinsed and drained
- 2 tablespoons cornstarch
- ½ cup light coconut milk
- 2 cloves garlic, minced
- 2 teaspoons ginger, minced
- ½ teaspoon red pepper flakes
- 1 teaspoon lime juice
- 3 teaspoons curry powder
- 2 tablespoons sugar
- Salt and pepper to taste

For serving

- Coconut flakes
- ¼ cup fresh basil, chopped
- Cooked rice

Instructions:

Transfer the pineapple juice from the can to a cup.

Add the pineapple chunks, chicken cubes, onion, sweet red pepper, carrots and chickpeas to your slow cooker.

In a bowl, mix the cornstarch, coconut milk, garlic, ginger, red pepper flakes, lime juice, curry powder, sugar, salt and pepper.

Stir in the reserved pineapple juice.

Pour the mixture over the chicken.

Cover the pot.

Cook on low for 8 hours.

Sprinkle with the coconut flakes and basil.

Serve with the rice.

Nutrients per Serving:

- Calories 395
- Fat 9.4 g
- Saturated Fat 4.7 g
- Cholesterol 0 mg
- Sugars 22.5 g
- Carbohydrate 66.9 g
- Fiber 15.4 g
- Protein 15.4 g
- Sodium 36 mg
- Potassium 909 mg

Coconut Curry Shrimp

Shrimp and sweet red pepper in coconut curry sauce—this is the dish that turns dinnertime into something special without wearing you out.

Serving Size: 3

Preparation & Cooking Time: 30 minutes

Ingredients:

- 2/3 cup coconut milk
- 1 ½ teaspoons curry powder
- 1 tablespoon fish sauce
- 1 teaspoon brown sugar
- Salt and pepper to taste
- 1 lb. shrimp, peeled and deveined
- 2 green onions, chopped
- 1 sweet red pepper, chopped
- ¼ cup fresh cilantro, minced

For serving

- Lime wedges
- Cooked rice

Instructions:

Mix the coconut milk, fish sauce, curry powder, brown sugar, salt and pepper in a bowl.

Add the shrimp to a pan over medium heat.

Take 2 tablespoons of the coconut milk mixture and add this to the pan.

Cook while stirring for 3 minutes.

Transfer to a plate.

Add the green onion and red pepper to the pan.

Pour in the remaining coconut milk mixture.

Bring to a boil.

Reduce heat and simmer for 3 minutes.

Put the shrimp back to the pan along with the cilantro.

Heat through for 2 minutes.

Garnish with the lime wedges.

Serve with the hot cooked rice.

Nutrients per Serving:

- Calories 256
- Fat 13 g
- Saturated fat 10 g
- Carbohydrates 8 g
- Fiber 2 g
- Protein 27 g
- Cholesterol 184 mg
- Sugars 4 g
- Sodium 841 mg
- Potassium 440 mg

Pork & Apple Curry

Apple in a curry dish? As it turns out, apples lend a unique flavor to a pork curry dish, and at the same time, provide a little crunch to keep things interesting.

Serving Size: 8

Preparation & Cooking Time: 5 hours and 45 minutes

Ingredients:

- 2 lb. pork loin roast, sliced into cubes
- 1 onion, chopped
- 1 clove garlic, minced
- 1 apple, diced
- 1 tablespoon curry powder
- ½ cup orange juice
- 1 teaspoon chicken bouillon granules
- ¼ teaspoon ground cinnamon
- ½ teaspoon ground ginger
- Salt to taste
- 2 tablespoons cold water
- 2 tablespoons cornstarch

For serving

- ¼ cup apple, diced
- ¼ cup coconut flakes, toasted
- ¼ cup raisins
- Hot cooked rice

Instructions:

Add the pork cubes, onion, garlic, apple, curry powder, orange juice, chicken bouillon granules, ground cinnamon, ground ginger and salt to your slow cooker.

Mix well.

Cover the pot.

Cook on low for 5 hours.

Combine the cold water and cornstarch in a bowl.

Add the mixture to the pot.

Seal the pot.

Cook on high for 30 minutes.

Stir in the apples.

Sprinkle the coconut flakes and raisins on top.

Serve with the hot cooked rice.

Nutrients per Serving:

- Calories 174
- Fat 6 g
- Saturated fat 2 g
- Carbohydrates 8 g
- Fiber 1 g
- Protein 22 g
- Cholesterol 57 mg
- Sugars 4 g
- Sodium 287 mg
- Potassium 479 mg

Lamb & Potato Curry

For a dish that's guaranteed to impress everyone, here's a recipe you can turn to—lamb and potatoes in curry sauce with tomatoes and spices.

Serving Size: 6

Preparation & Cooking Time: 8 hours and 30 minutes

Ingredients:

- 1 tablespoon olive oil
- 3 tablespoons curry powder, divided
- 6 cloves garlic, minced and divided
- 2 teaspoons garam masala, divided
- 2 tablespoons ginger, minced and divided
- 1 teaspoon dried thyme
- 1 teaspoon ground coriander, divided
- 1 teaspoon chili powder
- 1 teaspoon paprika
- Salt and pepper to taste
- ¼ teaspoon ground cumin
- 2 lb. lamb chops
- 4 red potatoes, diced
- 1 cup chicken broth
- 15 oz. canned diced tomatoes
- 1 onion, chopped

For serving

- Chopped fresh cilantro
- Cooked brown rice

Instructions:

Pour the olive oil into a bowl.

Stir in 1 tablespoon curry powder, half of the minced garlic, 1 teaspoon garam masala, half of minced ginger, dried thyme, paprika, chili powder, ½ teaspoon ground coriander, salt and pepper.

Mix well.

Stir in the lamb chops.

Cover and refrigerate for 4 hours.

Add the lamb and potatoes to your slow cooker.

Pour in the broth and tomatoes.

Sprinkle the onions and remaining garlic, ginger and spices on top.

Cover the pot.

Cook on low for 4 hours.

Chop the lamb.

Put the lamb back to the pot.

Serve with the rice and sprinkle with the cilantro.

Nutrients per Serving:

- Calories 337
- Fat 19 g
- Saturated fat 7 g
- Carbohydrates 21 g
- Fiber 5 g
- Protein 22 g
- Cholesterol 76 mg
- Sugars 4 g
- Sodium 935 mg
- Potassium 987 mg

Chicken & Corn Chowder Curry

This is a comforting soup dish that warms you up on chilly nights. To make this dish more flavorful, curry powder is added to chicken and corn chowder.

Serving Size: 8

Preparation & Cooking Time: 45 minutes

Ingredients:

- 1 tablespoon butter
- 2 celery ribs, chopped
- 2 onions, diced
- 2 teaspoons curry powder
- Pinch cayenne pepper
- Salt and pepper to taste
- 43 ½ oz. low sodium chicken broth
- 5 cups corn kernels
- ½ cup milk
- ½ cup all purpose flour
- 1/3 cup fresh cilantro, minced
- 3 cups chicken breast, sliced into cubes

Instructions:

Add the butter to a pan over medium heat.

Cook the celery and onions to the pan for 3 minutes, stirring often.

Stir in the curry power, cayenne pepper, salt and pepper.

Cook while stirring for 30 seconds.

Pour in the chicken broth and add the corn kernels.

Bring to a boil.

Reduce heat and simmer for 15 minutes.

In a bowl, mix the milk and flour.

Add this to the soup.

Return to a boil.

Reduce heat and simmer for 2 minutes.

Stir in the cilantro and chicken.

Nutrients per Serving:

- Calories 229
- Fat 4 g
- Saturated fat 2 g
- Carbohydrates 28 g
- Fiber 3 g
- Protein 22 g
- Cholesterol 45 mg
- Sugars 5 g
- Sodium 582 mg
- Potassium 430 mg

Vegetable Thai Curry Soup

This is another Thai curry dish that will turn you into a Thai cuisine fan. The broth is loaded with delicious flavors that make every sip a treat for your taste buds.

Serving Size: 6

Preparation & Cooking Time: 30 minutes

Ingredients:

- 8 oz. rice noodles
- 1 tablespoon sesame oil
- 2 tablespoons red curry paste
- 1 cup coconut milk
- 1 tablespoon low sodium soy sauce
- 32 oz. vegetable broth
- ½ sweet red pepper, sliced into strips
- 5 oz. bamboo shoots
- 1 ½ cups shiitake mushrooms, sliced
- 8 ¾ oz. baby corn, sliced in half
- 14 oz. tofu, sliced into cubes

Garnish

- Lime wedges
- Basil leaves

Instructions:

Prepare the rice noodles according to the directions in the package.

Pour the oil into a pot over medium heat.

Cook the curry paste for 30 seconds, stirring often.

Stir in the coconut milk, soy sauce and vegetable broth.

Bring to a boil.

Add the sweet red pepper, bamboo shoots, shiitake mushrooms, baby corn and tofu.

Cook for 5 minutes.

Add the noodles to the soup.

Transfer to serving bowls.

Serve with lime wedges and basil.

Nutrients per Serving:

- Calories 289
- Fat 9 g
- Saturated fat 3 g
- Carbohydrates 41 g
- Fiber 2 g
- Protein 11 g
- Cholesterol 0 mg
- Sugars 3 g
- Sodium 772 mg
- Potassium 567 mg

Tofu & Cauliflower Curry

This vegetarian dish is so appetizing even meat lovers can't enough of it. Tofu, cauliflower florets, chickpeas drenched in flavorful curry sauce and served with hot cooked rice.

Serving Size: 6

Preparation & Cooking Time: 30 minutes

Ingredients:

- 1 tablespoon olive oil
- 1 onion, chopped
- 2 carrots, diced
- 3 teaspoons curry powder
- Salt and pepper to taste
- 14 oz. tofu, sliced into cubes
- 3 cups cauliflower florets
- 1 cup vegetable broth
- 14 oz. canned tomatoes
- 1 cup green peas
- 15 oz. chickpeas, rinsed and drained
- 13 oz. coconut milk

For serving

- Fresh cilantro, chopped
- Hot cooked rice

Instructions:

Pour the oil into a pot over medium high heat.

Cook the onion and carrots for 5 minutes, stirring often.

Season with the curry powder, salt and pepper.

Stir in the tofu and cauliflower.

Pour in the vegetable broth and tomatoes.

Bring to a boil.

Reduce heat and simmer for 10 minutes.

Stir in the green peas, chickpeas and coconut milk.

Return to a boil.

Reduce heat and simmer for 5 minutes.

Sprinkle with the cilantro.

Serve with the hot cooked rice.

Nutrients per Serving:

- Calories 338
- Fat 21 g
- Saturated fat 13 g
- Carbohydrates 29 g
- Fiber 7 g
- Protein 13 g
- Cholesterol 0 mg
- Sugars 9 g
- Sodium 528 mg
- Potassium 335 mg

Caribbean Chicken Curry

Infuse your usual chicken curry dish with Caribbean flavors and everyone would surely be raving about it.

Serving Size: 8

Preparation & Cooking Time: 4 hours and 20 minutes

Ingredients:

- 1 teaspoon garlic powder
- 1 tablespoon Madras curry powder
- Pepper to taste
- 8 chicken thigh fillets
- 1 onion, sliced thinly
- 1 ½ cups Goya mojo criollo marinade
- 2 tablespoons vegetable oil
- 2 tablespoons all purpose flour

For serving

- Chopped cilantro
- Chopped green onion
- Cooked rice

Instructions:

Mix the garlic powder, curry powder and pepper in a bowl.

Sprinkle both sides of chicken with the mixture.

Add the chicken to your slow cooker.

Top with the onion.

Pour in the marinade.

Cover the pot.

Cook on low for 4 hours.

Take the chicken out of the pot.

Skim off the fat.

In a pan over medium heat, add the oil.

Stir in the flour and cooking juices.

Bring to a boil.

Reduce heat and simmer for 2 minutes.

Stir in the chicken.

Simmer for 5 minutes.

Sprinkle the chopped cilantro and green onions on top.

Serve with the hot cooked rice.

Nutrients per Serving:

- Calories 249
- Fat 13 g
- Saturated fat 3 g
- Carbohydrates 11 g
- Fiber 1 g
- Protein 22 g
- Cholesterol 76 mg
- Sugars 5 g
- Sodium 514 mg
- Potassium 238 mg

Red Chicken Curry

Don't worry if it's a busy day. Since this recipe is semi-homemade and makes use of convenient ingredients like pre-cut stir-fry vegetables, you get to save time and effort.

Serving Size: 4

Preparation & Cooking Time: 20 minutes

Ingredients:

- 1/3 cup chicken broth
- 13 oz. coconut milk
- 2 tablespoons fish sauce
- 1 tablespoon red curry paste
- 2 tablespoons brown sugar
- 3 cups chicken breast, cooked and sliced into cubes
- 2 cups frozen stir-fry vegetable mix

For serving

- Chopped cilantro
- Hot cooked rice

Instructions:

First, pour the chicken broth and coconut milk into a pan over medium heat.

Stir in the red curry paste, fish sauce and brown sugar.

Bring to a boil.

Reduce heat.

Next, simmer for 5 minutes.

Add the stir-fry vegetables to the pan.

Return to a boil.

Reduce the heat and then simmer for 10 minutes.

Stir in the chicken.

Cook for 3 more minutes.

Top with the cilantro and serve with the rice.

Nutrients per Serving:

- Calories 250
- Fat 23.2 g
- Saturated Fat 19.9 g
- Carbohydrate 10.7 g
- Fiber 2 g
- Protein 3 g
- Cholesterol 0 mg
- Sugars 7.8 g
- Sodium 968 mg
- Potassium 291 mg

Filipino-Style Chicken Curry

There are many ways to cook chicken curry, and this is one that will truly imprint a mark in your tummy! The difference is that the vegetables are cooked in oil prior to adding to the sauce.

Serving Size: 6

Preparation & Cooking Time: 1 hour

Ingredients:

- ¼ cup canola oil
- 2 potatoes, sliced into cubes
- 2 carrots, sliced into cubes
- 1 red bell pepper, diced
- 1 green bell pepper, diced
- 1 onion, sliced
- 1 small ginger, sliced into thin strips
- 3 cloves garlic, minced
- 3 lb. chicken
- 1 cup coconut milk
- 1 tablespoon fish sauce
- 1 cup water
- 2 tablespoons curry powder
- Salt and pepper to taste

Instructions:

Add the oil to a pan over medium heat.

Cook the potatoes for 3 minutes or until a little browned.

Drain the potatoes on a plate lined with paper towels.

Add the carrots to the same pan.

Cook for 2 minutes.

Drain on the same plate.

Remove the oil from the pan.

Cook the bell peppers for 30 seconds, stirring often.

Stir in the onion, ginger and garlic.

Add the chicken.

Cook until browned on all sides.

Pour in the coconut milk, fish sauce and water.

Bring to a boil.

Reduce heat and simmer for 20 minutes.

Stir in the curry powder, salt and pepper.

Cook for 3 more minutes.

Add the vegetables and serve.

Nutrients per Serving:

- Calories 602
- Fat 26 g
- Saturated Fat 11.1 g
- Carbohydrate 21.9 g
- Fiber 4.8 g
- Protein 69.1 g
- Cholesterol 175 mg
- Sugars 6.1 g
- Sodium 403 mg
- Potassium 1032 mg

Turkey & Cauliflower Curry

This turkey and cauliflower curry is a tasty meal that only takes 30 minutes or less to prepare. What makes this curry dish different from the others is the addition of mango chutney.

Serving Size: 6

Preparation & Cooking Time: 30 minutes

Ingredients:

- 1 1/3 cups chicken stock
- 3 cloves garlic, minced
- ½ teaspoon ground cardamom
- 2 tablespoons curry powder
- 2 tablespoons fresh cilantro, minced
- Salt and pepper to taste
- 1 onion, chopped
- 3 carrots, sliced thinly
- 16 oz. cauliflower florets
- 3 cups turkey, cooked and diced
- ½ cup mango chutney
- 1 cup coconut milk
- 2 teaspoons all purpose flour

For serving

- 4 ½ cups hot cooked rice
- Additional mango chutney

Instructions:

Pour the chicken stock into a pan over medium heat.

Stir in the garlic, curry powder, ground cardamom, cilantro, salt and pepper.

Mix well.

Add the onion and carrots.

Bring to a boil.

Reduce heat and simmer for 5 minutes.

Add the chutney and turkey.

Cook for 3 minutes.

Combine the coconut milk and flour in a bowl.

Add this mixture to the pan.

Return to a boil.

Reduce heat and simmer for 2 minutes.

Serve with the rice and additional mango chutney.

Nutrients per Serving:

- Calories 363
- Fat 9 g
- Saturated fat 7 g
- Carbohydrates 64 g
- Fiber 5 g
- Protein 7 g
- Cholesterol 1 mg
- Sugars 16 g
- Sodium 787 mg
- Potassium 714 mg

Spicy Chicken Curry

This spicy chicken curry dish is infused with authentic Indian flavors that you won't be able to resist.

Serving Size: 4

Preparation & Cooking Time: 45 minutes

Ingredients:

- 1 onion, sliced
- 3 tablespoons water
- 6 cloves garlic, chopped
- 2 teaspoons ginger, minced
- 4 tablespoons water
- 4 tablespoons vegetable oil
- 1 cinnamon stick
- 1 teaspoon fennel seeds
- 2 teaspoons cumin seeds
- 1 teaspoon red pepper flakes
- 1 teaspoon turmeric
- 1 teaspoon garam masala
- 4 cups canned tomatoes
- 4 cups chicken stock
- 8 chicken thigh fillets
- 2 tablespoons coriander, chopped
- 1 teaspoon sugar

Instructions:

Add the onion and water to your food processor.

Pulse until consistency is similar to a paste.

Transfer to a bowl.

Add the garlic and ginger to your food processor.

Pour in the water.

Process until consistency is similar to a paste.

Pour the vegetable oil into a pan over medium heat.

Add the cinnamon stick, fennel seeds, cumin seeds and red pepper flakes.

Cook while stirring for 30 seconds.

Add the onion and garlic-ginger paste.

Cook for 5 minutes.

Stir in the rest of the ingredients

Cook for 15 minutes.

Discard the cinnamon stick before serving.

Nutrients per Serving:

- Calories 196
- Fat 15.1 g
- Saturated Fat 2.9 g
- Carbohydrate 14.8 g
- Fiber 3.5 g
- Protein 3.3 g
- Cholesterol 0 mg
- Sugars 7.8 g
- Sodium 779 mg
- Potassium 565 mg

Chicken & Veggie Curry

Prepare this comforting chicken and vegetable curry for dinner if you don't have a lot of time to spare but want a delicious and healthy meal.

Serving Size: 4

Preparation & Cooking Time: 30 minutes

Ingredients:

- 1 ½ lb. chicken breast fillet, sliced into cubes
- 1 ¼ cups coconut milk
- Salt to taste
- 2 tablespoons red curry paste
- 16 oz. stir-fry vegetable mix
- 1 tablespoon olive oil

Instructions:

Preheat your oven to 425 degrees F.

Arrange the chicken in a baking pan.

In a bowl, mix the coconut milk, salt and curry paste.

Pour the mixture into the baking pan.

Bake in the oven for 20 minutes.

Stir fry the vegetables in olive oil for 5 minutes.

Serve the chicken curry with the vegetables.

Nutrients per Serving:

- Calories 511
- Fat 14 g
- Saturated fat 6 g
- Carbohydrates 51 g
- Fiber 5 g
- Protein 41 g
- Cholesterol 94 mg
- Sugars 6 g
- Sodium 606 mg
- Potassium 611 mg

Curry Pork Chops with Tomato

This dish is proof to the saying that simply doesn't have to be boring. Flavor up your pork chops with tomato, curry powder and spices, for a simple but appetizing dish that's also easy to prepare.

Serving Size: 6

Preparation & Cooking Time: 40 minutes

Ingredients:

- 4 teaspoons butter, divided
- 6 pork chops
- 1 onion, chopped
- 5 cups apples, sliced thinly
- 28 oz. canned tomatoes
- 2 teaspoons curry powder
- 4 teaspoons sugar
- ½ teaspoon chili powder
- Salt to taste

For serving

- 2 tablespoons almonds, toasted and slivered
- Hot cooked brown rice

Instructions:

Add half of the butter to a pan over medium heat.

Cook the pork chops until browned on both sides.

Transfer to a plate.

Add the remaining butter to the pan.

Cook the onion for 3 minutes, stirring often.

Add the apples and tomatoes.

Sprinkle with the curry powder, sugar, chili powder and salt.

Bring to a boil.

Add the pork chops back to the pan.

Reduce heat and simmer for 5 minutes.

Flip the pork chops.

Cook for another 3 to 5 minutes.

Top with the almonds and serve with the rice.

Nutrients per Serving:

- Calories 478
- Fat 14 g
- Saturated fat 5 g
- Carbohydrates 50 g
- Fiber 7 g
- Protein 38 g
- Cholesterol 89 mg
- Sugars 15 g
- Sodium 475 mg
- Potassium 830 mg

Cauliflower Curry with Chickpeas & Green Peas

If you find the yellow curry too strong, you can use green curry powder instead for a milder flavor. Try this with this cauliflower dish with chickpeas and green peas.

Serving Size: 6

Preparation & Cooking Time: 20 minutes

Ingredients:

- 13 oz. coconut milk
- ¼ cup green curry paste
- Salt to taste
- 30 oz. chickpeas, rinsed and drained
- 3 cups cauliflower florets
- 2 teaspoons cornstarch
- 1 tablespoon cold water
- 1 ½ cups green peas

For serving

- ½ cup cashews
- 4 cups cooked rice

Instructions:

Pour the coconut milk into a pan over medium heat.

Stir in the green curry paste and salt.

Once dissolved, add the chickpeas and cauliflower.

Bring to a boil.

Reduce heat and simmer for 5 minutes.

Mix the cornstarch and water in a bowl.

Add this to the pan.

Stir in the green peas.

Return to a boil.

Reduce heat and simmer for 2 minutes.

Sprinkle the cashews on top.

Serve with the rice.

Nutrients per Serving:

- Calories 516
- Fat 24 g
- Saturated fat 13 g
- Carbohydrates 63 g
- Fiber 10 g
- Protein 15 g
- Cholesterol 0 mg
- Sugars 7 g
- Sodium 646 mg
- Potassium 1442 mg

Curried Chicken Meatballs in Lettuce Wraps

Infuse your chicken meatballs with curry flavors and wrap them in lettuce leaves for a simple but delicious and healthy snack or dinner.

Serving Size: 24

Preparation & Cooking Time: 45 minutes

Ingredients:

- 1 lb. lean ground chicken
- 1 onion, minced
- 1 egg, beaten
- ¼ cup raisins
- 2 teaspoons curry powder
- ¼ cup fresh cilantro, minced
- Salt to taste

Sauce

- 1 cup plain Greek yogurt
- ¼ cup fresh cilantro, minced

Wraps

- 24 lettuce leaves
- ½ cup raisins
- 1 carrot, shredded
- ½ cup peanuts, chopped

Instructions:

Preheat your oven to 350 degrees F.

Add the lean ground chicken, onion, egg, raisins, curry powder, fresh cilantro and salt to a bowl. Mix well.

Shape the mixture into 24 balls.

Add the meatballs to a baking pan.

Bake in the oven for 20 minutes.

Combine the sauce ingredients in another bowl.

Top the lettuce leaves with the meatballs, yogurt sauce, raisins, shredded carrots and peanuts.

Nutrients per Serving:

- Calories 72
- Fat 3 g
- Saturated fat 1 g
- Carbohydrates 6 g
- Fiber 1 g
- Protein 6 g
- Cholesterol 22 mg
- Sugars 4 g
- Sodium 89 mg
- Potassium 54 mg

Curried Quinoa Salad

Quinoa salad is not only high in fiber and nutrients but is also a delicious and filling meal you'd love each time. To make it even more appetizing, we add curry flavor to the salad dressing.

Serving Size: 6

Preparation & Cooking Time: 2 hours and 40 minutes

Ingredients:

- 14 oz. vegetable broth
- 1 cup quinoa, rinsed and drained
- ¼ teaspoon ground cumin
- 1 teaspoon ground turmeric
- ¼ cup red onion, diced
- 1 ½ cups cherry tomatoes, sliced in half
- 1 cucumber, diced

Dressing

- 2 tablespoons olive oil
- 2 tablespoons lemon juice
- 1 teaspoon yellow mustard
- 1 tablespoon honey
- 1/8 teaspoon cayenne pepper
- ½ teaspoon curry powder
- Salt to taste

Instructions:

Pour the vegetable broth into a pan over medium heat.

Stir in the quinoa, ground cumin and ground turmeric.

Bring to a boil.

Reduce heat and simmer for 15 minutes.

Turn off heat.

Transfer the quinoa to a plate and let cool.

Toss the quinoa, onion, tomato and cucumber in a salad bowl.

Mix the salad dressing in another bowl.

Pour into the salad and mix.

Refrigerate for 2 hours.

Stir before serving.

Nutrients per Serving:

- Calories 176
- Fat 6 g
- Saturated fat 1 g
- Carbohydrates 25 g
- Fiber 3 g
- Protein 5 g
- Cholesterol 0 mg
- Sugars 5 g
- Sodium 320 mg
- Potassium 427 mg

Chicken Curry Turnovers

Curry powder definitely makes these chicken turnovers a lot more enticing. Be sure to prepare a big batch of these.

Serving Size: 8

Preparation & Cooking Time: 45 minutes

Ingredients:

- 1 cup chicken, cooked and chopped
- 1 green onion, minced
- ½ cup mayonnaise
- 1 apple, chopped
- ¼ cup cashews, chopped
- Salt and pepper to taste
- 2 teaspoons curry powder
- Pastry sheets
- 1 egg, beaten

Instructions:

Preheat your oven to 425 degrees F.

Mix the chicken, green onion, mayo, apple, cashews, salt, pepper and curry powder in a bowl.

Divide the pastry sheet into 8 pieces.

Top with the chicken mixture.

Fold and seal the edges.

Add the turnovers to a baking pan.

Brush the outside with the egg.

Make a slit on top of each turnover.

Bake in the oven for 20 minutes.

Nutrients per Serving:

- Calories 512
- Fat 37 g
- Saturated fat 17 g
- Carbohydrates 34 g
- Fiber 2 g
- Protein 11 g
- Cholesterol 101 mg
- Sugars 2 g
- Sodium 526 mg
- Potassium 508 mg

Rice & Noodle Curry

This is not your typical curry dish but you're going to be surprised at how tasty and satisfying this dish is.

Serving Size: 4

Preparation & Cooking Time: 30 minutes

Ingredients:

- 2 oz. angel hair pasta
- 2 eggs, beaten
- 1 tablespoon vegetable oil
- 2 cloves garlic, minced
- 1 sweet red pepper, chopped
- 1 summer squash, sliced thinly
- ¼ teaspoon red pepper flakes
- ½ teaspoon ground ginger
- 2 teaspoons curry powder
- 4 cups cooked rice
- 1 teaspoon sesame oil
- 1 tablespoon lime juice
- 2 tablespoons low sodium soy sauce
- ½ cup cashews, chopped
- 2 green onions, chopped

Instructions:

Prepare the pasta according to the directions in the package.

Drain and let cool.

Spray your pan with oil.

Add the pan over medium heat.

Cook the eggs until firm.

Transfer to a plate.

Pour the oil into a pan over medium high heat.

Add the garlic, red pepper and squash.

Stir in the red pepper flakes, ground ginger and curry powder.

Cook for 2 to 3 minutes.

Stir in the pasta and rice.

Drizzle with the sesame oil, lime juice and soy sauce.

Top with the cashews, cooked eggs and green onions.

Nutrients per Serving:

- Calories 360
- Fat 17 g
- Saturated fat 3 g
- Carbohydrates 38 g
- Fiber 4 g
- Protein 12 g
- Cholesterol 93 mg
- Sugars 4 g
- Sodium 449 mg
- Potassium 284 mg

Peach & Curried Chicken Salad

This is another flavorful salad recipe that makes use of curried chicken. Arugula, curried chicken and peaches make for an incredible salad dish that everyone would be amazed with.

Serving Size: 4

Preparation & Cooking Time: 10 minutes

Ingredients:

- 1 teaspoon curry powder
- ½ cup nonfat mayonnaise
- 2 cups chicken, cooked and sliced into cubes
- ¼ cup raisins
- ½ cup walnuts, chopped
- 5 oz. mixed salad greens
- 2 peaches, sliced

Instructions:

Add the curry powder and mayo to a bowl.

Mix well.

Stir in the chicken, raisins and walnuts.

Arrange the salad greens on a serving platter.

Top with the peaches and chicken mixture.

Nutrients per Serving:

- Calories 286
- Fat 12 g
- Saturated fat 2 g
- Carbohydrates 23 g
- Fiber 4 g
- Protein 24 g
- Cholesterol 54 mg
- Sugars 14 g
- Sodium 315 mg
- Potassium 492 mg

Potato & Chickpea Curry

The secret to this amazing Indian-inspired dish is sautéing first the onion, garlic and ginger until browned before cooking for long hours in the slow cooker.

Serving Size: 6

Preparation & Cooking Time: 6 hours and 30 minutes

Ingredients:

- 1 tablespoon vegetable oil
- 1 onion, chopped
- 2 cloves garlic, minced
- 2 teaspoons ginger, minced
- 1 teaspoon garam masala
- ¼ teaspoon ground turmeric
- ½ teaspoon ground cumin
- 2 teaspoons ground coriander
- 1 teaspoon chili powder
- 15 oz. canned crushed tomatoes
- 2 ½ cups vegetable stock
- 1 potato, sliced into cubes
- 30 oz. chickpeas, rinsed and drained
- 1 tablespoon lime juice

For serving

- Fresh cilantro, chopped
- Lime wedges
- Red onion, sliced
- Hot cooked rice

Instructions:

Pour the oil into a pan over medium high heat.

Cook the onion for 3 minutes, stirring often.

Add the garlic and ginger.

Cook for 30 seconds.

Stir in the garam masala, ground turmeric, ground coriander, ground cumin and chili powder.

Cook for 1 minute, stirring.

Pour in the tomatoes.

Cook for 2 minutes.

Transfer the mixture to your slow cooker.

Pour in the vegetable stock.

Add the potatoes and chickpeas.

Mix well.

Cover the pot.

Cook on low for 6 hours.

Add the lime juice.

Garnish with the fresh cilantro, lime wedges and red onion slices.

Serve with the hot cooked rice.

Nutrients per Serving:

- Calories 240
- Fat 6 g
- Saturated fat 0 g
- Carbohydrates 42 g
- Fiber 9 g
- Protein 8 g
- Cholesterol 0 mg
- Sugars 8 g
- Sodium 767 mg
- Potassium 713 mg

Coconut Red Curry Stew

This curry stew made with red curry paste is loaded with irresistible flavors that would make you crave for more. It's a good thing this stew only takes a few minutes of active preparation.

Serving Size: 4

Preparation & Cooking Time: 1 hour

Ingredients:

- 1 tablespoon canola oil
- 1 onion, chopped
- 1 clove garlic, minced
- ½ teaspoon sugar
- 3 tablespoons red curry paste
- 1 sweet red pepper, sliced
- 1 green pepper, sliced
- 15 oz. chickpeas, rinsed and drained
- 3 cups butternut squash, diced
- 4 cups eggplant, diced
- 32 oz. vegetable broth, divided
- 13 oz. coconut milk
- 15 oz. canned crushed tomatoes

For serving

- Fresh cilantro, chopped
- Lime wedges
- Hot cooked rice

Instructions:

Pour the oil into a pot over medium high heat.

Cook the onion for 3 minutes.

Stir in the garlic.

Cook while stirring for 1 minute.

Add the sugar and curry paste.

Stir in the sweet red pepper, green pepper, chickpeas, butternut squash and eggplant.

Pour in 3 cups of the broth, coconut milk and tomatoes.

Bring to a boil.

Reduce heat and simmer for 40 minutes.

Pour in the remaining broth.

Heat through for 5 minutes.

Top with the cilantro.

Serve with the lime wedges and hot cooked rice.

Nutrients per Serving:

- Calories 457
- Fat 22 g
- Saturated fat 16 g
- Carbohydrates 59 g
- Fiber 14 g
- Protein 11 g
- Cholesterol 0 mg
- Sugars 20 g
- Sodium 864 mg
- Potassium 976 mg

Curry Chicken & Rice

Add cashews and vegetables to your favorite chicken and rice dish to give it an extra crunch. Season it with curry powder or paste to make it even more appetizing.

Serving Size: 4

Preparation & Cooking Time: 30 minutes

Ingredients:

- 1 ¾ cups water
- 1 tablespoon olive oil
- 7 oz. rice pilaf mix
- 1 teaspoon curry powder
- 4 oz. green peas
- 14 ½ oz. canned diced tomatoes with chili
- 2 cups rotisserie chicken, cooked and shredded
- ½ cup cashews, roasted

Instructions:

Pour the water and oil into a pot over medium high heat.

Bring to a boil.

Stir in the rice mix and the curry powder.

Return to a boil.

Reduce heat.

Cover the pot and simmer for 15 minutes.

Stir in the green peas, diced tomatoes with chili and shredded chicken.

Cover and cook for 10 minutes.

Top with the cashews and serve.

Nutrients per Serving:

- Calories 500
- Fat 18 g
- Saturated fat 4 g
- Carbohydrates 53 g
- Fiber 5 g
- Protein 32 g
- Cholesterol 62 mg
- Sugars 6 g
- Sodium 1162 mg
- Potassium 522 mg

Slow Cooked Pork Curry

Slow cooked pork curry is a special dish that requires long hours of cooking, but thankfully only an hour or less of active preparation.

Serving Size: 10

Preparation & Cooking Time: 3 hours and 45 minutes

Ingredients:

- 1 ½ teaspoons curry powder
- ¾ teaspoon garlic powder
- ¾ teaspoon onion powder
- 1 teaspoon ground cumin
- ¼ teaspoon cayenne pepper
- 1 teaspoon dried oregano
- ¼ teaspoon ground chipotle pepper
- ¼ teaspoon paprika
- Salt and pepper to taste
- 14 ½ oz. low sodium chicken broth
- 3 cups butternut squash, sliced into cubes
- 4 carrots, sliced thinly
- 1 ½ lb. potatoes, sliced
- 4 lb. pork loin roast

Instructions:

Add the curry powder, onion powder, garlic powder, dried oregano, ground cumin, cayenne pepper, ground chipotle pepper, paprika, salt and pepper to a bowl. Mix well.

Pour the broth into your slow cooker.

Stir in the butternut squash, carrots and potatoes.

Pour 2 teaspoons of the spice mixture into the pot.

Rub the remaining spice mixture on all sides of the roast.

Place the roast on top of the vegetables.

Cover and cook on low for 3 hours and 30 minutes.

Let stand for 15 minutes before slicing the pork.

Serve the pork with the vegetables.

Nutrients per Serving:

- Calories 261
- Fat 7 g
- Saturated fat 2 g
- Carbohydrates 21 g
- Fiber 4 g
- Protein 29 g
- Cholesterol 68 mg
- Sugars 3 g
- Sodium 523 mg
- Potassium 691 mg

Egg Curry Salad Sandwich

Curried egg salad is a good idea to serve alongside main courses. You can also use this as a topping for your open-faced sandwich for a tasty and healthy snack.

Serving Size: 6

Preparation & Cooking Time: 15 minutes

Ingredients:

- ½ cup mayonnaise
- ½ teaspoon honey
- ½ teaspoon curry powder
- Pinch ground ginger
- 3 green onions, chopped
- 6 hard-boiled eggs, peeled and diced
- 6 slices whole wheat bread
- Tomato, sliced
- Pepper to taste

Instructions:

Combine the mayo, honey, curry powder and ground ginger in a bowl.

Mix well.

Stir in the green onion and eggs.

Top the bread slices with the egg salad mixture.

Add the tomatoes on top.

Sprinkle with the pepper before serving.

Nutrients per Serving:

- Calories 273
- Fat 20 g
- Saturated fat 4 g
- Carbohydrates 14 g
- Fiber 2 g
- Protein 10 g
- Cholesterol 188 mg
- Sugars 2 g
- Sodium 284 mg
- Potassium 179 mg

Sausage & Squash Curry

This quick and easy to sausage and squash curry is a breath of fresh air when you're running out of ideas to prepare for dinner.

Serving Size: 8

Preparation & Cooking Time: 35 minutes

Ingredients:

- 1 tablespoon olive oil
- 1 lb. Italian sausage, removed from casing and crumbled
- 1 onion, chopped
- 1 green bell pepper, diced
- 6 cups butternut squash, sliced into cubes
- 1 apple, sliced into cubes
- Salt to taste
- 2 teaspoons curry powder
- 3 cups pasta shells, cooked
- ¼ cup water

Instructions:

Pour the oil into a pan over medium heat.

Cook the sausage until browned.

Transfer to a plate lined with paper towels.

Add the onion and bell pepper to the same pan.

Cook for 3 minutes, stirring often.

Stir in the squash.

Cook while stirring for 5 minutes.

Stir in the apples.

Season with the salt and curry powder.

Cook for 3 minutes.

Put the sausage back to the pan.

Add the water and pasta shells.

Cook for 2 minutes.

Serve warm.

Nutrients per Serving:

- Calories 385
- Fat 18 g
- Saturated fat 5 g
- Carbohydrates 44 g
- Fiber 4 g
- Protein 14 g
- Cholesterol 38 mg
- Sugars 7 g
- Sodium 735 mg
- Potassium 722 mg

Shrimp & Pineapple Curried Fried Rice

Here's a different way of preparing fried rice. Not only will you add shrimp and pineapple to the fried rice to make it tastier and more filling, you can also spice things up with curry powder.

Serving Size: 4

Preparation & Cooking Time: 30 minutes

Ingredients:

- 1 teaspoon curry powder
- ½ teaspoon sugar
- 2 tablespoons soy sauce
- 2 tablespoons peanut oil, divided
- 1 lb. shrimp, peeled and deveined
- 1 clove garlic, minced
- 2 teaspoons ginger, minced
- ½ cup onion, chopped
- 1 sweet red pepper, chopped
- 1 carrot, chopped
- 20 oz. canned pineapple chunks
- 2 cups cooked rice, room temperature
- ½ cup peanuts, chopped
- 6 green onions, chopped

Instructions:

In a bowl, mix the curry powder, sugar and soy sauce.

Pour half of the peanut oil to a pan over medium high heat.

Cook the shrimp for 3 minutes, stirring often.

Transfer to a plate.

Add the remaining oil to the pan.

Cook the garlic and ginger for 20 seconds, stirring.

Stir in the onion, sweet red pepper and carrot.

Cook while stirring for 2 minutes.

Add the shrimp, pineapple, rice and curry mixture.

Cook while stirring for 5 minutes.

Sprinkle the peanuts and green onions on top.

Garnish with the lime wedges and serve.

Nutrients per Serving:

- Calories 491
- Fat 18 g
- Saturated fat 3 g
- Carbohydrates 54 g
- Fiber 5 g
- Protein 28 g
- Cholesterol 138 mg
- Sugars 22 g
- Sodium 513 mg
- Potassium 410 mg

Curried Beef Stew

This is a special beef stew that your family will describe as a labor of love. It takes quite a lot of work and long hours of cooking but in the end, every sip makes all the effort worth it.

Serving Size: 4

Preparation & Cooking Time: 4 hours

Ingredients:

- 3 lb. beef stew meat
- Salt and pepper to taste
- 2 tablespoons all purpose flour
- 1 tablespoon canola oil
- 1 onion, sliced
- 2 teaspoons low sodium soy sauce
- 3 cups beef stock
- 2 tablespoons curry powder
- 2 bay leaves
- 2 carrots, sliced
- 1 ½ lb. potatoes, sliced into cubes
- 1 tablespoon white vinegar

For serving

- Hot cooked brown rice

Instructions:

Season the beef cubes with the salt and pepper.

Coat the beef cubes with the flour.

Pour the oil into a pan over medium heat.

Cook the onion and beef until browned, stirring from time to time.

Stir in the soy sauce and curry powder.

Pour in the stock.

Add the bay leaves.

Stir well.

Bring to a boil.

Reduce heat.

Cover the pot and then simmer for 1 hour and 45 minutes.

Stir in the carrots and potatoes.

Return to a boil.

Reduce heat to low.

Simmer while covered for another 1 hour and 45 minutes, stirring from time to time.

Stir in the white vinegar.

Discard the bay leaves.

Serve with the hot cooked rice.

Nutrients per Serving:

- Calories 362
- Fat 10 g
- Saturated fat 3 g
- Carbohydrates 44 g
- Fiber 7 g
- Protein 24 g
- Cholesterol 53 mg
- Sugars 7 g
- Sodium 691 mg
- Potassium 410 mg

Chicken Curry Lasagna

Take your lasagna to a different level with this recipe that only takes you a little over an hour to prepare.

Serving Size: 12

Preparation & Cooking Time: 1 hour and 10 minutes

Ingredients:

- 1 tablespoon canola oil
- 1 onion, chopped
- 3 cloves garlic, minced
- 4 teaspoons curry powder
- 6 oz. tomato paste
- 26 oz. coconut milk
- 4 cups rotisserie chicken, cooked and shredded
- 12 lasagna noodles
- ½ cup fresh cilantro, chopped and divided
- 2 cups ricotta cheese
- 10 oz. spinach, chopped
- 2 eggs, beaten
- Salt and pepper to taste
- 2 cups mozzarella cheese, shredded

Instructions:

Preheat your oven to 350 degrees F.

Add the oil to a pan over medium high heat.

Cook the onion for 5 minutes.

Stir in the garlic and curry powder.

Cook while stirring for 1 minute.

Add the tomato paste and coconut milk.

Bring to a boil.

Reduce heat and simmer for 3 to 5 minutes.

Add the shredded chicken.

Prepare the lasagna noodles according to the directions in the package.

In a bowl, combine ¼ cup cilantro, ricotta cheese, spinach, eggs, salt and pepper.

Spread a layer of the chicken mixture into a baking pan.

Layer on top 4 lasagna noodles and ricotta mixture.

Repeat the layers.

Add the mozzarella cheese on top.

Bake in the oven for 40 minutes.

Let cool for 10 minutes before slicing.

Sprinkle the remaining cilantro on top and serve.

Nutrients per Serving:

- Calories 343
- Fat 17 g
- Saturated fat 11 g
- Carbohydrates 28 g
- Fiber 2 g
- Protein 20 g
- Cholesterol 68 mg
- Sugars 3 g
- Sodium 322 mg
- Potassium 529 mg

Curried Eggs & Rice

Not all special dishes take a lot of time and effort. This traditional Indian dish of curried eggs is one that's easy and simple to prepare but definitely ups the ante of your dinner.

Serving Size: 4

Preparation & Cooking Time: 35 minutes

Ingredients:

- 8 eggs, hard-boiled and sliced in half
- ¼ cup butter
- 1 onion, chopped
- 1 clove garlic, minced
- 2 teaspoons tomato paste
- 2 teaspoons curry powder
- 14 oz. canned diced tomatoes
- 1 cup water
- 1 teaspoon lemon juice
- 16 oz. cooked rice

Toppings

- Roasted peanuts
- Raisins
- Chutney
- Orange zest
- Coconut flakes

Instructions:

Add the butter to a pan over medium high heat.

Cook the onion for 5 minutes, stirring often.

Stir in the garlic.

Add the tomato paste and curry powder.

Cook for 30 seconds, stirring often.

Pour in the tomatoes and water.

Bring to a boil.

Reduce heat and simmer for 10 minutes.

Stir in the lemon juice.

Add the eggs.

Cook for 4 minutes.

Serve the eggs on top of the rice with the roasted peanuts, raisins, chutney, orange zest and coconut flakes.

Nutrients per Serving:

- Calories 464
- Fat 24 g
- Saturated fat 10 g
- Carbohydrates 43 g
- Fiber 2 g
- Protein 17 g
- Cholesterol 403 mg
- Sugars 1 g
- Sodium 236 mg
- Potassium 475 mg

Chicken Tikka Masala

This homemade chicken tikka masala will make you want to go back for a second serving. This traditional Indian dish is made by cooking marinated chicken in spicy curry sauce.

Serving Size: 4

Preparation & Cooking Time: 3 hours and 30 minutes

Ingredients:

- 1 tablespoon olive oil
- 1 onion, grated
- 3 cloves garlic, minced
- 1 teaspoon curry powder
- 2 tablespoons tomato paste
- 15 oz. tomato puree
- 1 tablespoon lemon juice
- 1 teaspoon lemon zest
- 1 teaspoon hot pepper sauce
- ¼ teaspoon garam masala
- Salt and pepper to taste
- 4 chicken thigh fillets
- 1 tablespoon butter, melted
- 3 tablespoons plain Greek yogurt

For serving

- Lemon zest
- Fresh cilantro, chopped
- Hot cooked rice

Instructions:

Add the olive oil, onion, garlic, curry powder, tomato paste, tomato puree, lemon juice, lemon zest, hot pepper sauce, garam masala, salt and pepper to your slow cooker.

Mix well.

Stir in the chicken thighs.

Cover the pot.

Cook on low for 3 hours.

Preheat your broiler.

Transfer the chicken to a broiler pan.

Broil the chicken for 3 minutes per side.

Pour the cooking juice into a pan over medium high heat.

Cook for 7 minutes.

Stir in the butter and yogurt.

Pour the sauce over the chicken.

Garnish with the lemon zest and cilantro.

Serve with the hot cooked rice.

Nutrients per Serving:

- Calories 364
- Fat 22 g
- Saturated fat 7 g
- Carbohydrates 12 g
- Fiber 3 g
- Protein 25 g
- Cholesterol 91 mg
- Sugars 4 g
- Sodium 705 mg
- Potassium 612 mg

Crispy Curry Chicken

You'll love how these chicken drumsticks are crispy on the outside and tender inside. These are also packed with delicious flavors that would make you wish you prepared more.

Serving Size: 4

Preparation & Cooking Time: 1 hour and 10 minutes

Ingredients:

- 1 lb. chicken drumsticks
- 2 tablespoons olive oil
- ½ teaspoon onion salt
- ½ teaspoon garlic powder
- 2 teaspoons curry powder
- Salt to taste
- Chopped cilantro

Instructions:

Preheat your oven to 400 degrees F.

In a bowl, mix the olive oil, onion salt, garlic powder, curry powder and salt.

Brush both sides of the chicken with the mixture.

Arrange the chicken in a single layer on a baking pan.

Bake in the oven for 1 hour, flipping halfway through.

Sprinkle with the fresh cilantro before serving.

Nutrients per Serving:

- Calories 180
- Fat 13 g
- Saturated fat 3 g
- Carbohydrates 1 g
- Fiber 1 g
- Protein 15 g
- Cholesterol 47 mg
- Sugars 0 g
- Sodium 711 mg
- Potassium 245 mg

Chicken Curry Zucchini Noodle Soup

This is another comforting chicken noodle soup dish that's made more flavorful with the addition of curry. Also, instead of using the usual noodles, we use zucchini noodles for this recipe.

Serving Size: 8

Preparation & Cooking Time: 50 minutes

Ingredients:

- 2 tablespoons olive oil, divided
- 1 lb. chicken breast fillet, sliced into cubes
- 1 red onion, chopped
- 2/3 cup carrots, sliced
- 1 clove garlic, minced
- 2 tablespoons ginger, grated
- 1 star anise
- 1 lemongrass stalk
- 3 bay leaves
- 2 teaspoons ground turmeric
- ¼ teaspoon cayenne pepper
- 1 tablespoon curry powder
- Salt to taste
- 2 tablespoons white wine vinegar
- 14 oz. coconut milk
- 32 oz. chicken broth
- 2 tablespoons brown sugar
- ½ cup cherry tomatoes, sliced in half
- 1 ½ cups fresh kale, chopped
- 6 oz. zucchini, sliced into thin strips and steamed

Instructions:

Pour 1 tablespoon olive oil into a pan over medium heat.

Cook the chicken for 5 minutes, stirring frequently.

Transfer to a plate lined with paper towel.

Add the remaining olive oil.

Cook the onion and carrots for 12 minutes, stirring often.

Stir in the garlic, ginger, star anise, lemongrass, bay leaves, ground turmeric, curry powder, cayenne pepper and salt.

Cook for 1 minute, stirring often.

Pour in the vinegar.

Deglaze the pan by stirring the browned bits using a wooden spoon.

Pour in the coconut milk and broth.

Add the sugar.

Bring to a boil.

Reduce heat.

Add the tomatoes and kale.

Simmer for 5 minutes.

Discard the lemongrass, star anise and bay leaves.

Add the chicken and zucchini noodles.

Heat through for 3 minutes.

Nutrients per Serving:

- Calories 316
- Fat 16 g
- Saturated fat 11 g
- Carbohydrates 26 g
- Fiber 2 g
- Protein 15 g
- Cholesterol 46 mg
- Sugars 6 g
- Sodium 758 mg
- Potassium 671 mg

Eggplant Curry

This vegetarian dish is not only a cinch to prepare but also healthy and full of enticing flavors.

Serving Size: 2

Preparation & Cooking Time: 40 minutes

Ingredients:

- 1 tablespoon olive oil
- 1 eggplant, diced
- 1 red onion, minced
- 2 cloves garlic, minced
- 1 teaspoon curry powder
- 1 teaspoon turmeric
- 1 teaspoon ground coriander
- 14 oz. canned tomatoes
- 1 ½ cups coconut milk
- Salt and pepper to taste

Instructions:

Pour the olive oil into a pan over medium high heat.

Cook the eggplant for 3 minutes, stirring often.

Stir in the onion and garlic.

Cook for 2 minutes, stirring often.

Add the rest of the ingredients.

Cover the pan.

Reduce heat and simmer for 15 minutes.

Nutrients per Serving:

- Calories 601
- Fat 51.1 g
- Saturated Fat 39.2 g
- Carbohydrate 38.6 g
- Fiber 16.2 g
- Protein 9.1 g
- Cholesterol 0 mg
- Sugars 20.5 g
- Sodium 45 mg
- Potassium 1605 mg

Curry Roast Chicken

Roast chicken is a popular centerpiece in dinner parties. We make roast chicken more interesting by seasoning it with curry powder and other spices. For sure, everyone will take notice.

Serving Size: 6 to 8

Preparation & Cooking Time: 2 hours and 15 minutes

Ingredients:

- 4 tablespoons coconut oil, divided
- ½ teaspoon granulated garlic
- 2 teaspoons curry powder
- Salt to taste
- 1 whole chicken
- Pepper to taste
- 3 green onions, chopped
- 1 celery rib, chopped
- 1 lemon, sliced into wedges
- 1 cup leeks, chopped
- 1 cup low sodium chicken broth

Gravy

- 1 tablespoon butter
- 1 tablespoon all purpose flour
- 1 cup low sodium chicken broth
- ½ cup white wine

Garnish

- Lemon slices
- Chives, chopped
- Parsley, chopped

Instructions:

Preheat your oven to 350 degrees F.

Add 2 tablespoons coconut oil to a bowl.

Stir in the garlic, curry powder and salt.

Rub the mixture all over the chicken.

Sprinkle all sides with pepper.

Rub the inside of the chicken with the remaining coconut oil.

Toss the green onion, celery, lemon wedges and leeks in a bowl.

Stuff the chicken with this mixture.

Tie the drumsticks together to hold the stuffing.

Place the chicken on a roasting pan.

Roast in the oven for 45 minutes.

Pour in the chicken broth.

Roast for another 1 hour.

Pour the cooking liquid into a pan over medium heat.

Stir in the gravy ingredients.

Bring to a boil.

Reduce heat and simmer until gravy has thickened.

Serve the chicken with the gravy.

Garnish with the lemon slices, chives and parsley.

Nutrients per Serving:

- Calories 580
- Fat 38 g
- Saturated fat 17 g
- Carbohydrates 6 g
- Fiber 1 g
- Protein 49 g
- Cholesterol 154 mg
- Sugars 2 g
- Sodium 1328 mg
- Potassium 315 mg

Creamy Vegetable Curry

This is both a vegetable stew and a curry dish. You're going to love it not only for its bright colors, but also its irresistible aroma and burst-in-your-mouth flavors.

Serving Size: 6

Preparation & Cooking Time: 7 hours and 30 minutes

Ingredients:

- 2 cups fresh mushrooms
- 2 cups asparagus, trimmed and steamed
- 6 red potatoes, sliced into cubes
- 2 cups baby carrots
- 5 green onions, minced
- 1 ½ cups green peas
- 1 ½ cups corn kernels
- 2 tablespoons curry powder
- 30 oz. curry sauce
- 1 ½ teaspoons ground mustard
- 2 teaspoons garam masala
- ¼ cup fresh parsley, chopped

For serving

- Hot cooked rice
- Naan flatbreads

Instructions:

Add the fresh mushrooms, asparagus, potatoes, carrots, green onions, green peas and corn kernels to your slow cooker.

Toss to combine.

In a bowl, mix the curry powder, curry sauce, ground mustard, and garam masala.

Add this mixture to the pot.

Cover the pot.

Cook on low for 7 hours.

Sprinkle with the parsley.

Serve with the rice or naan flatbread.

Nutrients per Serving:

- Calories 455
- Fat 20 g
- Saturated fat 10 g
- Carbohydrates 61 g
- Fiber 11 g
- Protein 11 g
- Cholesterol 5 mg
- Sugars 18 g
- Sodium 495 mg
- Potassium 1412 mg

Chicken & Sweet Potato Curry

This curry dish is a delectable combination of sweet, spicy, and savory flavors. It takes hours of cooking but the preparation is minimal.

Serving Size: 8

Preparation & Cooking Time: 5 hours and 45 minutes

Ingredients:

- 2 lb. chicken thigh fillets
- 1 teaspoon granulated garlic
- 2 teaspoons curry powder
- Salt to taste
- 2 tablespoons canola oil
- 2 sweet potatoes, sliced into cubes
- 1 onion, chopped
- ½ cup apricot preserves
- ½ cup pineapple preserves
- 8 oz. canned pineapple chunks
- 1 tablespoon soy sauce
- 2 tablespoons cornstarch
- 1 tablespoon water
- Fresh parsley, chopped

Instructions:

Season both sides of the chicken with the garlic, curry powder and salt.

Add the oil to a pan over medium heat.

Cook the chicken for 3 minutes per side.

Add the onion and sweet potatoes to a slow cooker.

Place the chicken on top.

Add the fruit preserves and pineapple chunks on top.

Drizzle with the soy sauce.

Cover the pot.

Cook on low for 5 hours.

In a bowl, mix the cornstarch and water.

Stir into the slow cooker.

Cover and cook on high for 20 minutes.

Sprinkle with the chopped parsley and serve.

Nutrients per Serving:

- Calories 383
- Fat 8 g
- Saturated fat 2 g
- Carbohydrates 55 g
- Fiber 3 g
- Protein 23 g
- Cholesterol 76 mg
- Sugars 31 g
- Sodium 352 mg
- Potassium 246 mg

Butter Chicken

Butter chicken is another traditional Indian dish that's popular in the United States and many other countries. But you don't have to be a kitchen pro to cook this surprisingly simple dish.

Serving Size: 8

Preparation & Cooking Time: 3 hours and 10 minutes

Ingredients:

- 2 tablespoons butter
- 1 onion, chopped
- 4 cloves garlic, sliced thinly
- 1 teaspoon ground ginger
- ½ teaspoon chili powder
- 2 teaspoons red curry powder
- 2 teaspoons garam masala
- 2 tablespoons whole wheat flour
- 1 tablespoon olive oil
- 14 oz. coconut milk
- ¼ cup tomato paste
- Salt and pepper to taste
- 3 lb. chicken breast fillets, sliced into cubes

For serving

- Fresh cilantro leaves
- Hot cooked rice

Instructions:

Add the butter to a pan over medium high heat.

Cook the onion for 2 minutes.

Stir in the garlic and ginger.

Cook for 1 minute.

Season with the chili powder, red curry powder and garam masala.

Cook for another 1 minute.

Stir in the flour.

Add the olive oil.

Mix until paste is formed.

Stir in the tomato paste and coconut milk.

Cook for 2 minutes.

Season with the salt and pepper.

Transfer the mixture to a food processor.

Process until pureed.

Add the chicken and pureed mixture to the slow cooker.

Stir to coat evenly with the sauce.

Cover the pot.

Cook on low for 4 hours.

Sprinkle with the cilantro.

Serve with the hot cooked rice.

Nutrients per Serving:

- Calories 242
- Fat 9 g
- Saturated fat 3 g
- Carbohydrates 4 g
- Fiber 1 g
- Protein 35 g
- Cholesterol 102 mg
- Sugars 1 g
- Sodium 407 mg
- Potassium 332 mg

Curry Sausages

Yes, you can cook sausages in curry flavored sauce! Pair it up with potato fries for a snack or appetizer that's tasty and filling.

Serving Size: 4

Preparation & Cooking Time: 55 minutes

Ingredients:

- 1 tablespoon olive oil
- 1 lb. bratwursts, cooked and sliced
- 1 onion, chopped
- 2 cups ketchup
- ½ cup chicken broth
- 2 tablespoons curry powder
- 4 tablespoons red wine vinegar
- 2 tablespoons smoked paprika
- ¼ cup brown sugar
- French fries, cooked

Instructions:

Pour the olive oil into a pan over medium heat.

Add the bratwursts.

Cook for 5 minutes.

Stir in the onion.

Cook for another 5 minutes, stirring often.

In a bowl, mix the remaining ingredients, except the French fries.

Pour the mixture into the pan.

Bring to a boil.

Reduce heat and simmer for 10 minutes.

Serve with the French fries.

Nutrients per Serving:

- Calories 612
- Fat 37 g
- Saturated fat 12 g
- Carbohydrates 56 g
- Fiber 3 g
- Protein 17 g
- Cholesterol 85 mg
- Sugars 47 g
- Sodium 2611 mg
- Potassium 1256 mg

Turkey & Sweet Potato Curry

Turkey and sweet potato turn out to be a fantastic combination for a curry dish.

Serving Size: 6

Preparation & Cooking Time: 5 hours and 30 minutes

Ingredients:

- 1 tablespoon olive oil
- 1 onion, chopped
- 1 lb. ground turkey
- 2 cups chicken broth
- 4 oz. green chili, chopped
- 15 oz. sweet potato puree
- 1 teaspoon garlic powder
- ½ teaspoon dried oregano
- 1 tablespoon chili powder
- 1 teaspoon curry powder
- 1 teaspoon ground cumin
- Salt to taste
- 15 oz. great northern beans, rinsed and drained

For serving

- Red onion, sliced
- Fresh cilantro
- Sour cream

Instructions:

Pour the olive oil into a pan over medium heat.

Add the onion and turkey.

Cook until the turkey is browned and onion is soft.

Transfer the mixture to your slow cooker.

Pour in the chicken broth.

Stir in the green chili, sweet potato puree, garlic powder, dried oregano, chili powder, curry powder, ground cumin and salt.

Cover the pot.

Cook on low for 5 hours.

Stir in the beans.

Cook for 1 hour.

Top with the red onion, cilantro and sour cream before serving.

Nutrients per Serving:

- Calories 243
- Fat 6 g
- Saturated fat 1 g
- Carbohydrates 27 g
- Fiber 7 g
- Protein 20 g
- Cholesterol 52 mg
- Sugars 5 g
- Sodium 606 mg
- Potassium 750 mg

Conclusion

Cooking your own curry dishes at home is a gateway to a delightful journey through diverse tastes, fresh ingredients and endless combinations of flavors that may surprise you.

You'll find that curry is so much more than just spice and heat. It could also be healthy, easy and personalized meals.

Equipped with the right tools such as a straightforward cookbook and an open mind, you're well on your way to replicating some of your favorite restaurant favorites without having to splurge on takeout and food delivery.

Now isn't that a win-win?

About the Author

A native of Albuquerque, New Mexico, Sophia Freeman found her calling in the culinary arts when she enrolled at the Sante Fe School of Cooking. Freeman decided to take a year after graduation and travel around Europe, sampling the cuisine from small bistros and family owned restaurants from Italy to Portugal. Her bubbly personality and inquisitive nature made her popular with the locals in the villages and when she finished her trip and came home, she had made friends for life in the places she had visited. She also came home with a deeper understanding of European cuisine.

Freeman went to work at one of Albuquerque's 5-star restaurants as a sous-chef and soon worked her way up to head chef. The restaurant began to feature Freeman's original dishes as specials on the menu and soon after, she began to write e-books with her recipes. Sophia's dishes mix local flavours with European inspiration making them irresistible to the diners in her restaurant and the online community.

Freeman's experience in Europe didn't just teach her new ways of cooking, but also unique methods of presentation. Using rich sauces, crisp vegetables and meat cooked to perfection, she creates a stunning display as well as a delectable dish. She has won many local awards for her cuisine and she continues to delight her diners with her culinary masterpieces.

Author's Afterthoughts

I want to convey my big thanks to all of my readers who have taken the time to read my book. Readers like you make my work so rewarding and I cherish each and every one of you.

Grateful cannot describe how I feel when I know that someone has chosen my work over all of the choices available online. I hope you enjoyed the book as much as I enjoyed writing it.

Feedback from my readers is how I grow and learn as a chef and an author. Please take the time to let me know your thoughts by leaving a review on Amazon so I and your fellow readers can learn from your experience.

My deepest thanks,

Sophia Freeman

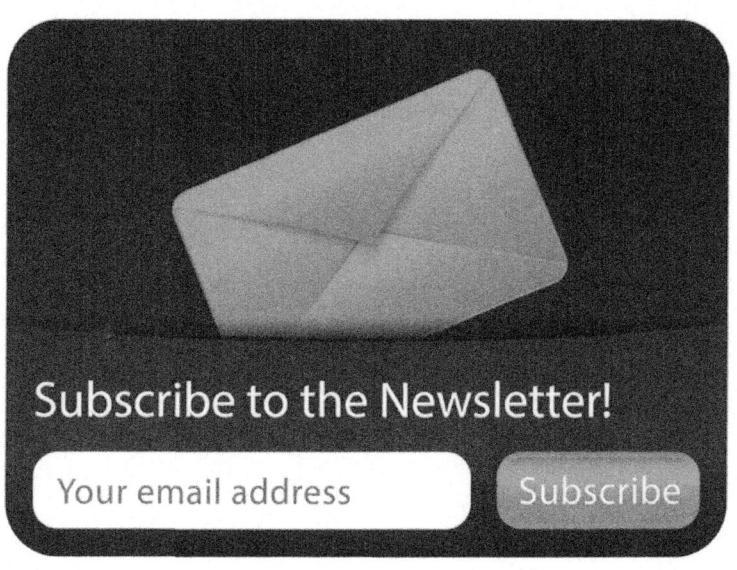

https://sophia.subscribemenow.com/

Printed in Great Britain
by Amazon